CHRIST'S BODY

Th
Community
of the King

HOWARD SNYDER

WITH ROBBIE & BRECK CASTLEMAN

**6 studies
for individuals or groups**

CHRISTIAN BASICS BIBLE STUDIES

With Guidelines for
Leaders & Study Notes
NIV Text Included

IVP

InterVarsity Press
Downers Grove, Illinois, USA
Leicester, England

InterVarsity Press
P.O. Box 1400, Downers Grove, IL 60515, USA
38 De Montfort Street, Leicester LE1 7GP, England

*InterVarsity Press® is the book-publishing division of InterVarsity Christian Fellowship®, a student
movement active on campus at hundreds of universities, colleges and schools of nursing in the
United States of America, and a member movement of the International Fellowship of Evangelical
Students. For information about local and regional activities, write Public Relations Dept.,
InterVarsity Christian Fellowship, 6400 Schroeder Rd., P.O. Box 7895, Madison, WI 53707-7895.*

*All Scripture quotations, unless otherwise indicated, are taken from the HOLY BIBLE, NEW
INTERNATIONAL VERSION®. NIV®. Copyright ©1973, 1978, 1984 by International Bible Society.
Used by permission of Zondervan Publishing House. All rights reserved.*

This study guide is based on and adapts material from The Community of the King *© 1977 by
InterVarsity Christian Fellowship of the United States of America.*

*Inter-Varsity Press, England, is the book-publishing division of the Universities and Colleges
Christian Fellowship (formerly the Inter-Varsity Fellowship), a student movement linking
Christian Unions in universities and colleges throughout the United Kingdom and the Republic of
Ireland, and a member movement of the International Fellowship of Evangelical Students. For
information about local and national activities write to UCCF, 38 De Montfort Street, Leicester
LE1 7GP.*

Cover photograph: Michael Goss

Cover background: Cowgirl Stock Photography ©1991

USA ISBN 0-8308-2016-7
UK ISBN 0-85111-375-3

Printed in the United States of America ♾

21	20	19	18	17	16	15	14	13	12	11	10	9	8	7	6	5	4	3	2	1
13	12	11	10	09	08	07	06	05	04	03	02	01	00	99	98	97	96			

Getting the Most Out of Christian Basics Bible Studies

Knowing Christ is where faith begins. From there we grow through the essentials of discipleship: Bible study, prayer, worship, Christian community and much more. We learn to set godly priorities, overcome spiritual opposition and witness to others. These are the topics woven into each of the Christian Basics Bible Studies. Working through this series will help you become a more mature Christian.

What Kind of Guide Is This?
The studies are not designed to merely tell you what one person thinks. Instead, through inductive study, they will help you discover for yourself what Scripture is saying. Each study deals with a particular passage—rather than jumping around the Bible—so that you can really delve into the author's meaning in that context.

The studies ask three different kinds of questions. *Observation* questions help you to understand the content of the passage by asking about the basic facts: who, what, when, where and how. *Interpretation* questions delve into the meaning of the passage. *Application* questions help you discover its implications for growing in Christ. These three keys unlock the treasures of the biblical writings and help you live them out.

This is a thought-provoking guide. Each question assumes a variety of answers. Many questions do not have "right" answers, particularly questions that aim at meaning or application. Instead, the questions should inspire users to explore the passage more thoroughly.

This study guide is flexible. You can use it for individual study, but it is also great for a variety of groups—student, professional, neighborhood or church groups. Each study takes about forty-five minutes in a group setting or thirty minutes in personal study.

How They're Put Together

Each study is composed of four sections: opening paragraphs and questions to help you get into the topic, the NIV text and questions that invite study of the passage, questions to help you apply what you have learned, and a suggestion for prayer.

The workbook format provides space for writing a response to each question. This format is ideal for personal study and allows group members to prepare in advance for the discussion and/or write down notes during the study. This space can form a permanent record of your thoughts and spiritual progress.

At the back of the guide are study notes which may be useful for leaders or for individuals. These notes do not give "the answers," but they do provide additional background information on certain questions to help you through the difficult spots. The

"Guidelines for Leaders" section describes how to lead a group discussion, gives helpful tips on group dynamics and suggests ways to deal with problems which may arise during the discussion. With such helps, someone with little or no experience can lead an effective group study.

Suggestions for Individual Study

1. If you have not read the book or booklet suggested in the "further reading" section, you may want to read the portion suggested before you begin your study.

2. Read the introduction. Consider the opening questions and note your responses.

3. Pray, asking God to speak to you from his Word about this particular topic.

4. Read the passage reproduced for you in the New International Version. You may wish to mark phrases that seem important. Note in the margin any questions that come to your mind as you read.

5. Use the questions from the study guide to more thoroughly examine the passage. Note your findings in the space provided. After you have made your own notes, read the corresponding study notes in the back of the book for further insights.

6. Reread the entire passage, making further notes about its general principles and about the way you intend to use them.

7. Move to the "commit" section. Spend time prayerfully considering what the passage has to say specifically to your life.

8. Read the suggestion for prayer. Speak to God about insights you have gained. Tell him of any desires you have for specific growth. Ask him to help you as you attempt to live out the principles described in that passage.

Suggestions for Members of a Group Study

Joining a Bible study group can be a great avenue to spiritual growth. Here are a few guidelines that will help you as you participate in the studies in this guide.

1. These studies focus on a particular passage of Scripture—in depth. Only rarely should you refer to other portions of the Bible, and then only at the request of the leader. Of course, the Bible is internally consistent. Other good forms of study draw on that consistency, but inductive Bible study sticks with a single passage and works on it in depth.

2. These are discussion studies. Questions in this guide aim at helping a group discuss together a passage of Scripture in order to understand its content, meaning and implications. Most people are either natural talkers or natural listeners. Yet this type of study works best if people participate more or less evenly. Try to curb any natural tendency to either excessive talking or excessive quiet. You and the rest of the group will benefit.

3. Most questions in this guide allow for a variety of answers. If you disagree with someone else's comment, gently say so. Then explain your own point of view from the passage before you.

4. Be willing to lead a discussion, if asked. Much of the preparation for leading has already been accomplished in the writing of this guide.

5. Respect the privacy of people in your group. Many people speak of things within the context of a Bible study/prayer group that they do not want to be public knowledge. Assume that personal information spoken within the group setting is private, unless you are specifically told otherwise. And don't talk about it elsewhere.

6. We recommend that all groups follow a few basic guidelines and that these guidelines be read at the first session. The guidelines, which you may wish to adapt to your situation, are the following:

a. Anything said in this group is considered confidential and will not be discussed outside the group unless specific permission is given to do so.

b. We will provide time for each person present to talk if he or she feels comfortable doing so.

c. We will talk about ourselves and our own situations, avoiding conversation about other people.

d. We will listen attentively to each other.

e. We will pray for each other.

7. Enjoy your study. Prepare to grow. God bless.

Suggestions for Group Leaders

There are specific suggestions to help you in leading in the guidelines for leaders and in the study notes at the back of this guide. Read the guidelines for leaders carefully, even if you are only leading one group meeting. Then you can go to the section on the particular session you will lead.

Introduction: Kingdom Agents

The church is the community of God's people—a people called to serve him and live together in true Christian community as a witness to the character and values of his kingdom. The church is the agent of God's mission on earth.

What is that mission? It is nothing other than bringing all things and, supremely, all people of the earth under the dominion and headship of Jesus Christ. If not all come willingly, nevertheless, every knee will bow and every tongue will confess that Jesus Christ is Lord (Philippians 2:10-11).

But to say the church is the agent of God's mission on earth is equivalent to saying the church is the agent of the kingdom of God. The church is the messianic community—the community of those who recognize the true Messiah, already confess him as Lord and proclaim his good news to the ends of the earth.

So *the church is the agent of the kingdom of God*. To speak of either the evangelistic or prophetic role of the church without relating these to the church's kingdom mission is to lose the biblical perspective and develop a truncated vision of the church's calling. Biblically, neither evangelism nor social action make full sense divorced from the fact of the Christian community as the visible, earthly expression of the kingdom of God.

The church is the only divinely appointed means for spreading the gospel. The gospel call is a call to *something*, and that something is more than a doctrine or an experience or a heavenly juridical transaction or the exercise of faith or even, exclusively, Jesus Christ. The gospel intends to call persons *to the body of Christ*, that is, the community of believers with Jesus Christ as its essential and sovereign head.

Look at what Jesus said and did. He spoke of the kingdom; he gathered the church. He did not say much about the church, and he refused to set up the kind of kingdom people expected. Instead he spoke of the "mystery" of the kingdom. Through his life, death, resurrection and visitation at Pentecost he established not the kingdom but the church, the community entrusted with living and proclaiming the mystery of the kingdom to the ends of the earth.

Jesus speaks of "the mystery of the kingdom"; Paul speaks of "the mystery of Christ." For Christ is the key to the kingdom. The kingdom of God is the ongoing reconciling work of God in Christ seen from the perspective of the final definitive establishment of God's dominion when Christ returns to earth. Christ must return to fully establish his kingdom. But by his Spirit he now works on earth through his body, the church.

How should the church and the kingdom be understood in these days between Jesus' first and second comings? These studies will lead you into a deeper understanding of the relationship between the kingdom and the church and what your place is in that.

For further reading: introduction and chapters one and two of The Community of the King. *(This guide builds on ideas outlined in* The Community of the King. *Recommended reading at the end of each study points you to the appropriate section of that book.)*

Study One
God's Master Plan

Ephesians 1:3-14, 22-23

I believe that God is saving souls and preparing them for heaven, but I would never accept that as an adequate definition of the church's mission. It is much too narrow. It is not a biblical definition, for the Bible speaks of a divine master plan for the whole creation. To be biblical we must see the church and the gospel within the context of God's cosmic plan.

What is this cosmic plan? It is stated most concisely in the first three chapters of Ephesians. Two striking facts emerge from these chapters. First, God has a plan and purpose. Second, this plan extends to the whole cosmos.

Open

☐ From recent news stories and headlines, what problems would you like to see God solve now?

☐ Think about personal or family problems you face. What would you like to see God solve now?

☐ What evidence do you have that God is presently at work in the world?

in your personal life and family?

Study

Read Ephesians 1:3-14, 22-23:

³Praise be to the God and Father of our Lord Jesus Christ, who has blessed us in the heavenly realms with every spiritual blessing in Christ. ⁴For he chose us in him before the creation of the world to be holy and blameless in his sight. In love ⁵he predestined us to be adopted as his sons through Jesus Christ, in accordance with his pleasure and will—⁶to the praise of his glorious grace, which he has freely given us in the One he loves. ⁷In him we have redemption through his blood, the forgiveness of sins, in accordance with the riches of God's grace ⁸that he lavished on us with all wisdom and understanding. ⁹And he made known to us the

mystery of his will according to his good pleasure, which he purposed in Christ, [10]to be put into effect when the times will have reached their fulfillment—to bring all things in heaven and on earth together under one head, even Christ.

[11]In him we were also chosen, having been predestined according to the plan of him who works out everything in conformity with the purpose of his will, [12]in order that we, who were the first to hope in Christ, might be for the praise of his glory. [13]And you also were included in Christ when you heard the word of truth, the gospel of your salvation. Having believed, you were marked in him with a seal, the promised Holy Spirit, [14]who is a deposit guaranteeing our inheritance until the redemption of those who are God's possession—to the praise of his glory. . . .

[22]And God placed all things under his feet and appointed him to be head over everything for the church, [23]which is his body, the fullness of him who fills everything in every way.

---

1. When did God conceive his master plan for the cosmos (v. 4)?

---

2. In verse 11 the Greek word sometimes translated "plan" comes from the word for "house" or "household." What is God's system of management for his household, the church?

3. What parts of the cosmos are included in God's master plan of reconciliation (vv. 10, 22-23)?

4. How is the salvation of individuals related to the reconciliation of all the created cosmos?

5. The testimony of Scripture is consistent: the same God who created the universe as perfect and sustains it will restore all things through the work of Christ. How does Paul summarize the work of Christ?

6. The church is the people of the kingdom of God living under and proclaiming God's rule. What is the role of the church in cosmic redemption?

7. When does God accomplish his work? One branch of the church has said, "Not now; then!" And, in reaction, another group has said, "Not then—now!" In light of the global, personal and family perspective you have noted, when do you expect God's solutions to be applied—"then" or "now"? Why?

Commit

☐ How can you more fully engage in Christ's work of cosmic reconciliation by your participation in the work and witness of the church?

For further reading: chapter three of The Community of the King.

Study Two
God's Reconciling Love

Ephesians 3:1-13

A remarkable phrase occurs in Ephesians 3:10. God's cosmic plan, Paul says, is that "through the church, the manifold wisdom of God should be made known to the rulers and authorities in the heavenly realms."

This passage reveals that Gentiles as well as Jews may share in God's promised redemption. In fact Jew and Gentile are brought together into "one body." Through Jesus Christ, God has "made the two one and has destroyed the barrier, the dividing wall of hostility." So all Christians are one body. This was "through the cross, by which he put to death their hostility" (Ephesians 2:14, 16).

Note the two dimensions here. Jewish and Gentile believers are reconciled both to God and to each other. They have joined in a reconciling relationship to Jesus that transcends and destroys their old hostility toward each other. No longer enemies, they are now brothers and sisters.

What then is the mystery of God's plan? It is that in Christ God acts with such redemptive power that he is able to overcome hatreds and heal hostilities. The mystery is not merely that the gospel is preached to Gentiles; it is that through this preaching Gentile believers are now "heirs together" and "members of one body."

Was the miracle of the gospel exhausted by the reconciliation of Jew and Gentile in the first century A.D.? Certainly not! There is more to the mystery of God's plan. That initial, historic reconciliation shows us that God reconciles alienated persons and peoples to himself through the blood of the cross. It extends to us today.

Open

☐ What "dividing walls of hostility" are evident in the church today?

☐ What evidence do you see that God is still working to reconcile people both to himself and to each other?

☐ In what areas of your personal and corporate church life do you need to experience reconciliation?

Study

Read Ephesians 3:1-13:

[1]For this reason I, Paul, the prisoner of Christ Jesus for the sake of you Gentiles—

[2]Surely you have heard about the administration of God's grace that was given to me for you, [3]that is, the mystery made known to me by revelation, as I have already written briefly. [4]In reading this, then, you will be able to understand my insight into the mystery of Christ, [5]which was not made known to men in other generations as it has now been revealed by the Spirit to God's holy apostles and prophets. [6]This mystery is that through the gospel the Gentiles are heirs together with Israel, members together of one body, and sharers together in the promise in Christ Jesus.

[7]I became a servant of this gospel by the gift of God's grace given me through the working of his power. [8]Although I am less than the least of all God's people, this grace was given me: to preach to the Gentiles the unsearchable riches of Christ, [9]and to make plain to everyone the administration of this mystery, which for ages past was kept hidden in God, who created all things. [10]His intent was that now, through the church, the manifold wisdom of God should be made known to the rulers and authorities in the heavenly realms, [11]according to his eternal purpose which he accomplished in Christ Jesus our Lord. [12]In him and through faith in him we may approach God with freedom and confidence. [13]I ask you, therefore, not to be discouraged because of my sufferings for you, which are your glory.

1. What is the "mystery of Christ" (vv. 4-6)?

How has it been revealed?

---

2. What two dimensions of reconciliation are accomplished through the work of Christ?

---

3. How is the church involved in revealing the "manifold wisdom" of God (vv. 10-11)?

---

4. How is the church the agent of God's will for others in the world?

for the creation?

---

5. How does the healthy or unhealthy community life of the church influence how the church fulfills its mission?

6. Since the church is the people of God, it includes all God's people in all times and in all places. How should this rich historical and cultural truth influence your local congregational community?

7. How is the Holy Spirit involved in making the church God's reconciling agent?

Commit

☐ What specifically can you do to strengthen the mission of your local congregation to be more effective agents of reconciliation?

Who can you ask to be a part of this effort?

For further reading: chapter four of The Community of the King.

Study Three
Ministering Together

1 Corinthians 12:4-13, 27-31

*T*here are spiritual truths I will never grasp and Christian standards I will never attain except as I share in community with other believers. This is God's plan. The Holy Spirit ministers to us, in large measure, through each other.

This has immediate implications for evangelism. The individual believer's responsibility is first of all to the Christian community and to its head, Jesus Christ. The first task of every Christian is the edification of the community of believers. If we say that reaching non-Christians is the first task of the believer, we are ignoring what the New Testament teaches about spiritual gifts and place a burden on the backs of some believers that they are not able to bear. Further, it puts all the emphasis at the one point of conversion and undervalues the upbuilding of the church, which is essential for effective evangelism and church growth.

This leads us to affirm the priority of community in relation to witness. Fellowship and community life are necessary within the church in order to equip Christians for their various kinds of witness and service. In one way or another all Christians are witnesses in the world and must share their faith. But we can be effective witnesses only as we experience the enabling common life of the church. And this common life is truly enabling only as the community becomes, through the indwelling of Christ and the exercise of spiritual gifts, the koinonia of the Holy Spirit.

Open

☐ In the body of Christ, who are the members you would most like to be like and why?

☐ What do you do to make the most significant contribution to the local body of Christ?

☐ What can you do to be more content and fruitful in your place within the body of Christ?

Study

Read 1 Corinthians 12:4-13, 27-31:

⁴There are different kinds of gifts, but the same Spirit. ⁵There are different kinds of service, but the same Lord. ⁶There are different kinds of working, but the same God works all of them in all men.

⁷Now to each one the manifestation of the Spirit is given for the common good. ⁸To one there is given through the Spirit the message of wisdom, to another the message of knowledge by means of the same Spirit, ⁹to another faith by the same Spirit, to another gifts of healing by that one Spirit, ¹⁰to another miraculous powers, to another prophecy, to another distinguishing between spirits, to another speaking in different kinds of tongues, and to still another the interpretation of tongues. ¹¹All these are the work of one and the same Spirit, and he gives them to each one, just as he determines.

¹²The body is a unit, though it is made up of many parts; and though all its parts are many, they form one body. So it is with Christ. ¹³For we were all baptized by one Spirit into one body—whether Jews or Greeks, slave or free—and we were all given the one Spirit to drink. . . .

²⁷Now you are the body of Christ, and each one of you is a part of it. ²⁸And in the church God has appointed first of all apostles, second prophets, third teachers, then workers of miracles, also those having gifts of healing, those able to help others, those with gifts of administration, and those speaking in different kinds of tongues. ²⁹Are all apostles? Are all prophets? Are all teachers? Do all work miracles? ³⁰Do all have gifts of healing? Do all speak in tongues? Do all interpret? ³¹But eagerly desire the greater gifts.

And now I will show you the most excellent way.

1. Verse 3 says, "No one can say, 'Jesus is Lord' except by the Holy Spirit." How does the exercise of the Spirit's gifts enable the church today to declare the lordship of Christ in the world?

2. Gifts must be seen not as spiritual fringe benefits but as completely central to the life experience and functioning of the Christian community. How is each of the gifts in verses 8-11 central to the community and not a fringe benefit?

3. How do these gifts contribute to the two directions of spiritual gifts: *outward* ministry in the world and *inward* ministry within the church?

4. In the New Testament there is no hierarchy of value or hint of a "ladder" concerning the Spirit's gifts (vv. 4-6, 12-13). How can each person's gifts within a community be equally valued?

5. How has your church shown (or how can it better show) that your gifts are appreciated and to be used?

6. How can the organization and order of the church *enhance* the exercise of each believer's gift and faith?

How can a church's organization and order *undermine* the exercise of gifts in the faith community?

7. How can you encourage those who minister to the body of Christ by the exercise of their gifts?

Commit

☐ Since gifts are given to meet the needs of a certain faith community and the area of the world in which the community is located, what spiritual gifts are needed in your church for its witness, work and fellowship?

☐ Plan to talk to someone in your church who knows you well and ask what gifts of the Spirit they see in you. Ask this person for prayerful advice and accountability as you exercise this gift. Talk with an elder or pastor about the results of this assessment.

For further reading: chapter five of The Community of the King.

Study Four
Bearing Witness

1 Peter 2:4-12

*T*he role of the church is both evangelistic and prophetic, without being exclusively one or the other. In one sense evangelism is good news and prophecy is bad news. Evangelism proclaims the offer of forgiveness, new life in Christ and new lifestyle in Christian community. Prophecy proclaims that even if this offer is rejected, God is still sovereign and will finally establish his kingdom in righteousness and in judgment. Evangelism is the offer of present salvation; prophecy is the assurance of final judgment.

The evangelistic task is not merely the task of individual believers but is a function of the church as the community of God's people. The evangelistic task of the church is to proclaim the good news of salvation in Jesus Christ throughout the world, making disciples and building the church. It is to fulfill the Great Commission of Matthew 28:19-20, Mark 16:15 and Acts 1:8. Although the role of the church in God's plan does not end with the evan-

gelistic task, it begins here. Reaching the world with the good news
depends on this task's being carried out.

Open

☐ What situations in another's life make you most aware of that
person's need for the gospel?

☐ In what setting are you most uncomfortable trying to witness to
another person about Jesus?

☐ Do you find yourself called to or involved in evangelism or
prophecy more often? Why?

Study

Read 1 Peter 2:4-12:

⁴As you come to him, the living Stone—rejected by men but
chosen by God and precious to him—⁵you also, like living stones,
are being built into a spiritual house to be a holy priesthood,
offering spiritual sacrifices acceptable to God through Jesus
Christ. ⁶For in Scripture it says: "See, I lay a stone in Zion, a
chosen and precious cornerstone, and the one who trusts in him

will never be put to shame." [7]Now to you who believe, this stone is precious. But to those who do not believe, "The stone the builders rejected has become the capstone," [8]and, "A stone that causes men to stumble and a rock that makes them fall." They stumble because they disobey the message—which is also what they were destined for.

[9]But you are a chosen people, a royal priesthood, a holy nation, a people belonging to God, that you may declare the praises of him who called you out of darkness into his wonderful light. [10]Once you were not a people, but now you are the people of God; once you had not received mercy, but now you have received mercy.

[11]Dear friends, I urge you, as aliens and strangers in the world, to abstain from sinful desires, which war against your soul. [12]Live such good lives among the pagans that, though they accuse you of doing wrong, they may see your good deeds and glorify God on the day he visits us.

1. What contrasts are made in this passage between the people of God and those living outside of the "cornerstone" of Jesus Christ?

2. What is the purpose of God's work in history (vv. 4-8)?

3. What has God done to bring his purposes to pass?

4. How do the descriptions of the church in verses 5 and 9 highlight the "community" nature of God's people?

5. What words of "good news" in this passage should be included in the church's evangelistic message?

6. In verses 7-12 what is the "bad news" to be included in the church's prophetic message?

7. How is the church to carry out its evangelistic and prophetic roles (vv. 9-12)?

8. In what ways is the sovereignty of God affirmed in this passage?

Commit

☐ If you were asked to design a class on evangelism for your local church, what ideas from this passage would you emphasize and why?

☐ What practical steps would help equip and motivate you to be a better witness?

__ attending an evangelism training workshop

__ changing relationship patterns to develop friendships with those outside the faith

__ better and more focused prayer for the lost

__ other_____

What is the first step you will take this week?

For further reading: chapter six of The Community of the King.

Study Five
Growing the Church

Matthew 13:24-33

*B*ooks, videos and speakers everywhere offer plans for church growth. Are these programs the church should embrace or reject?

When faithful to the gospel, the church through its growth furthers the cause of the kingdom. *But a word of warning!* If we confuse institutional church structures with the authentic church of Jesus Christ, we may be deceived into equating institutional church success with kingdom growth. This is a lie and a deception and leads to idolatry.

But God has called his church to make disciples of all peoples throughout all lands, and this implies numerical growth. Disciples are countable. Thus we have the startling and yet very matter-of-fact recording of numerical growth in the book of Acts. Luke gives us enough statistics to show that when the Spirit acts, the church grows numerically, but not enough to allow us to seize on numerical growth as the essence of the church or as the only measure of a church's life and effectiveness. In the parables he told, Jesus shows us how to maintain a biblical balance.

Open

☐ What have you read or heard about church growth that attracts you, and what turns you off?

☐ If you were to pick a congregation you have visited or read about as a model for church growth, which one would it be and why?

☐ What do you consider the clearest indications of a growing church?

Study

Read Matthew 13:24-33:

[24]Jesus told them another parable: "The kingdom of heaven is like a man who sowed good seed in his field. [25]But while everyone was sleeping, his enemy came and sowed weeds among the wheat, and went away. [26]When the wheat sprouted and formed heads, then the weeds also appeared.

[27]"The owner's servants came to him and said, 'Sir, didn't you sow good seed in your field? Where then did the weeds come from?'

[28] 'An enemy did this,' he replied.

"The servants asked him, 'Do you want us to go and pull them up?'

[29] 'No,' he answered, 'because while you are pulling the weeds, you may root up the wheat with them. [30]Let both grow together until the harvest. At that time I will tell the harvesters: First collect the weeds and tie them in bundles to be burned; then gather the wheat and bring it into my barn.' "

[31]He told them another parable: "The kingdom of heaven is like a mustard seed, which a man took and planted in his field. [32]Though it is the smallest of all your seeds, yet when it grows, it is the largest of garden plants and becomes a tree, so that the birds of the air come and perch in its branches."

[33]He told them still another parable: "The kingdom of heaven is like yeast that a woman took and mixed into a large amount of flour until it worked all through the dough."

1. What do these three parables illustrate?

2. What characteristics do the parables have in common?

3. How is the importance of measurable growth illustrated in each of these three parables?

_____

4. According to the parable of the weeds, why is numerical growth not a valid measurement of a church's life and effectiveness?

_____

5. How does the parable of the mustard seed encourage you to be faithful to the gospel?

_____

6. In what ways is the distinction between institutional growth and spiritual growth affirmed in the parable of the yeast and the dough?

_____

7. What encouragement can those in a church setting that is not seeing numerical growth draw from the parable of the mustard seed and the parable of the yeast and the dough?

8. Considering these parables, what do you think is God's role in making disciples and growing the church?

What is the role of the church?

Commit ————————————————————————————————
☐ From these parables, what advice would you give to someone in either a large growing church or a small church not seeing numerical growth?

☐ What is something you can do or are doing to serve your church as you reach out to others?

For further reading: chapter seven of The Community of the King.

Study Six
Organizing the Church

Acts 2:42-47

*O*nce upon a time there was a man named Bill who was fed up with the institutional church. "The church is so locked in to tradition," he said, "that no spiritual freedom can exist." So Bill gathered a small group of like-minded friends together. "We're going to throw out all the institutionalism and have a simple, unstructured, New Testament church," said Bill.

They all got together one Sunday evening. Eleven of them. They spent about two and a half hours just sharing, singing, praying and studying the Bible. It was great! Everyone was excited. This was the first time most of them had experienced such free, open fellowship, and the group felt drawn together and spiritually strengthened.

As it came time to break up that evening, Bill said, "Well, this has really been great! I think we've got something started here. Can we meet again next week?" Everyone agreed. Same time, same place.

And so a new fellowship—in effect, a new local church—was born. The group grew, diversified somewhat and met various needs as they arose. What about child care? What about time and length of meetings? What about leadership? What about special holiday observances? What about the cost of materials? In each case, ongoing, fixed arrangements were worked out so the group could function smoothly and would not have to keep making the same minor decisions all over again.

It worked. The group prospered.

But was it unstructured? Of course not! It inevitably took on institutional form. Perhaps the forms adopted were good forms; perhaps they were much better than those which had been left behind and better served the true purpose of the church. Probably so. But structures did indeed appear, for all life must have form. Life without form perishes because it cannot sustain itself. So how should the church be organized? Acts 2:42-47 gives us an interesting glimpse of the New Testament structure.

Open

☐ What tradition in your local church do you most appreciate?

☐ What church tradition would you most like to change?

☐ How do you think the changes you would make would be an

improvement in how the church functions in its work and witness?

Study

Read Acts 2:42-47:

⁴²They devoted themselves to the apostles' teaching and to the fellowship, to the breaking of bread and to prayer. ⁴³Everyone was filled with awe, and many wonders and miraculous signs were done by the apostles. ⁴⁴All the believers were together and had everything in common. ⁴⁵Selling their possessions and goods, they gave to anyone as he had need. ⁴⁶Every day they continued to meet together in the temple courts. They broke bread in their homes and ate together with glad and sincere hearts, ⁴⁷praising God and enjoying the favor of all the people. And the Lord added to their number daily those who were being saved.

1. What activities made up the worship of the church?

How are these activities evident in your church's worship?

2. What things defined the church's fellowship?

How are these things evident in your church's fellowship?

3. What was included in the church's ministry of compassion?

How are these included in your church's work and outreach?

4. What activities supported the evangelism of the church?

How are these activities evident in your church's witness to the gospel?

5. Note the roles the leadership played in the life of the church (vv. 42-43). How would these affect the church's structure?

6. Which of the church's activities were probably spontaneous, and which were planned?

How would those choices be an advantage to its life and witness?

Commit ───────────────────────────────────

☐ How we respond to the local church may depend to some extent on personality. Some of us are highly organized, and others strive on spontaneity. What structural (organizational) parts of the church's activities do you find most helpful to your spiritual life and why?

In what way do you need spontaneity in order to flourish spiritually?

☐ What change could you make in your church life that would help you spiritually or enable you to better serve?

Learning what to attempt to change and what to learn to appreciate can be a big struggle. Thank God for the things about your church you enjoy. Ask God to show you how he wants to use you there.

For further reading: chapters eight and nine of The Community of the King. *Also see the epilogue, which lists seven key steps you can take toward renewal.*

Guidelines for Leaders

Leading a Bible discussion can be an enjoyable and rewarding experience. But it can also be intimidating—especially if you've never done it before. If this is how you feel, you're in good company.

Remember when God asked Moses to lead the Israelites out of Egypt? Moses replied, "O Lord, please send someone else to do it" (Exodus 4:13). But God gave Moses the help (human and divine) he needed to be a strong leader.

Leading a Bible discussion is not difficult if you follow certain guidelines. You don't need to be an expert on the Bible or a trained teacher. The suggestions listed below can help you to effectively fulfill your role as leader—and enjoy doing it.

Preparing for the Study

1. As you study the passage ahead of time, ask God to help you understand it and apply it in your own life. Unless this happens, you will not be prepared to lead others. Pray too for the various members

of the group. Ask God to open your hearts to the message of his Word and motivate you to action.

2. Read the introduction to the entire guide to get an overview of the subject at hand and the issues which will be explored.

3. Be ready for the "Open" questions with a personal story or example. The group will be only as vulnerable and open as its leader.

4. As you begin preparing for each study, read and reread the assigned Bible passage to familiarize yourself with it. You may want to look up the passage in a Bible so that you can see its context.

5. This study guide is based on the New International Version of the Bible. That is what is reproduced in your guide. It will help you and the group if you use this translation as the basis for your study and discussion.

6. Carefully work through each question in the study. Spend time in meditation and reflection as you consider how to respond.

7. Write your thoughts and responses in the space provided in the study guide. This will help you to express your understanding of the passage clearly.

8. It might help you to have a Bible dictionary handy. Use it to look up any unfamiliar words, names or places. (For additional help on how to study a passage, see chapter five of *Leading Bible Discussions*, IVP.)

9. Take the final (application) questions and the "Commit" portion of each study seriously. Consider what this means for your life, what changes you may need to make in your lifestyle and/or what actions you can take in your church or with people you know. Remember that the group will follow your lead in responding to the studies.

Leading the Study

1. Be sure everyone in your group has a study guide and Bible. Encourage the group to prepare beforehand for each discussion by reading the introduction to the guide and by working through the questions in the study.

2. At the beginning of your first time together, explain that these studies are meant to be discussions, not lectures. Encourage the members of the group to participate. However, do not put pressure on those who may be hesitant to speak during the first few sessions.

3. Begin the study on time. Open with prayer, asking God to help the group understand and apply the passage.

4. Have a group member read the introductory paragraph at the beginning of the discussion. This will remind the group of the topic of the study.

5. Every study begins with a section called *Open*. These "approach" questions are meant to be asked before the passage is read. They are important for several reasons.

First, there is always a stiffness that needs to be overcome before people will begin to talk openly. A good question will break the ice.

Second, most people will have lots of different things going on in their minds (dinner, an exam, an important meeting coming up, how to get the car fixed) that have nothing to do with the study. A creative question will get their attention and draw them into the discussion.

Third, approach questions can reveal where our thoughts or feelings need to be transformed by Scripture. That is why it is especially important not to read the passage before the approach question is asked. The passage will tend to color the honest reactions people would otherwise give, because they feel they are supposed to think the way the Bible does.

6. Have a group member read aloud the passage to be studied.

7. As you ask the questions, keep in mind that they are designed to be used just as they are written. You may simply read them aloud. Or you may prefer to express them in your own words.

There may be times when it is appropriate to deviate from the study guide. For example, a question may already have been answered. If so, move on to the next question. Or someone may raise an important question not covered in the guide. Take time to discuss it, but try to keep the group from going off on tangents.

8. Avoid answering your own questions. Repeat or rephrase them if necessary until they are clearly understood. An eager group quickly becomes passive and silent if members think the leader will give all the *right* answers.

9. Don't be afraid of silence. People may need time to think about the question before formulating their answers.

10. Don't be content with just one answer. Ask, "What do the rest of you think?" or, "Anything else?" until several people have given answers to a question.

11. Acknowledge all contributions. Be affirming whenever possible. Never reject an answer. If it is clearly off-base, ask, "Which verse led you to that conclusion?" or, "What do the rest of you think?"

12. Don't expect every answer to be addressed to you, even though this will probably happen at first. As group members become more at ease, they will begin to truly interact with each other. This is one sign of healthy discussion.

13. Don't be afraid of controversy. It can be stimulating! If you don't resolve an issue completely, don't be frustrated. Move on and keep it in mind for later. A subsequent study may solve the problem.

14. Periodically summarize what the group has said about the passage. This helps to draw together the various ideas mentioned and gives continuity to the study. But don't preach.

15. Don't skip over the application questions at the end of each study. It's important that we each apply the message of the passage to ourselves in a specific way. Be willing to get things started by describing how you have been affected by the study.

Depending on the makeup of your group and the length of time you've been together, you may or may not want to discuss the "Commit" section. If not, allow the group to read it and reflect on it silently. Encourage members to make specific commitments and to write them in their study guide. Ask them the following week how they did with their commitments.

16. Conclude your time together with conversational prayer. Ask for God's help in following through on the commitments you've made.

17. End on time.

Many more suggestions and helps are found in *The Big Book on Small Groups, Small Group Leaders' Handbook* and *Good Things Come in Small Groups* (IVP). Reading through one of these books would be worth your time.

Study Notes

Study One. God's Master Plan. Ephesians 1:3-14, 22-23.
Purpose: To recognize God's plan of redemption for the whole creation and the purpose of the church as a part of that redemption.
Open. These questions are designed to help in identifying our expectations of God and how his redemptive plan for the entire cosmos is far greater and more inclusive than the perimeters of our personal experience.
Question 1. The same Greek word for *household* can be found in Ephesians 2:19.
Question 2. *Economics* is an English word derived from this Greek idea of household. It is important to recognize the full scope of all that God includes in his plan of redemption. God cares for the house and neighborhood as well as the people who live there. God cares for the entire lake and ecosystem, not just the fish!
Question 4. The key idea is that of reconciliation. God's plan is for the restoration of his creation, for overcoming, in glorious fulfillment, the damage done to persons and nature through the Fall. The redemption of persons is in the *center* of God's plan, but it is not the *circumference* of that plan.
Question 7. Those who postpone any real presence of the kingdom until after Christ's return ("Not now; *then!*") expect substantial renewal now only in the realm of individual religious experience, not in politics, art, education or culture in general, and not even really

in the church. On the other side are those who so emphasize present social renewal that both personal conversion and the space-time future return of Christ are denied or overshadowed, and our deep sinfulness and rebellion are not taken seriously. Our hope should be that orthodox Christians throughout the world can come to see that the kingdom of God is neither entirely present nor entirely future.

Study Two. God's Reconciling Love. Ephesians 3:1-13.

Purpose: To appreciate the completeness of God's plan to reconcile all creation to himself and all peoples to each other in Christ.

Open. Consider how you may or may not have experienced the effects of disunity within the body of Christ. Whom do you resist being reconciled with? It is important to consider the corporate nature of the church in God's work of reconciliation. The individual autonomy that often influences the church in democratic societies needs to be recognized in the light of the body of Christ as "one body with many members." Our corporate identity as one body of believers is of primary importance.

Questions 1-2. The reconciliation of all in Christ is why Paul can say that now "through the church, the manifold wisdom of God" is "made known to the rulers and authorities in the heavenly realms" (Ephesians 3:10). If the church is the *body* of Christ—the means of the head's action in the world—then the church is an indispensable part of the gospel. To adopt an "antichurch" position would dilute, even deny, the very gospel itself.

On question 2 you may also want to look at Ephesians 2:14-16.

Question 3. The church is the fruit of Christ's reconciling love, and thus the revelation of God's manifold wisdom. The church, as Christ's body, shares Christ's reconciling work.

Question 4. The church is more than God's agent of evangelism or social change; it is, in submission to Christ, the agent of God's entire cosmic purpose. What God is doing in Jesus Christ and what he is doing in and through the church are part of the redemption of all creation.

Question 5. The church must be seen as related to God's kingdom purposes. The Bible shows the church in the midst of culture, struggling to be faithful but sometimes adulterated by unnatural alliances. In Scripture the earthly and heavenly sides of the church fit together in one whole. You may want to consider Ephesians 1:3; 2:6 and 3:10 in considering how community health effects the kingdom.

Question 7. See also Ephesians 3:16-19.

Study Three. Ministering Together. 1 Corinthians 12:4-13, 27-31.

Purpose: To value the upbuilding of the church through each believer's contribution to the whole community of faith.

Question 1. The early Christian affirmation that "Jesus is Lord" must be the cry of the church today. The church as "the bride" and "the body" of Christ is a new reality in the world called to demonstrate the true character of the coming kingdom.

Question 2. In Ephesians spiritual gifts form the connecting link between Paul's statement of God's cosmic plan for the church and his description of normal church life. There is a link between foreordained "good works" (see Ephesians 2:10) and spiritual gifts, for it is principally through the exercise of spiritual gifts that each believer accomplishes those good works which make up God's cosmic plan.

Question 3. Spiritual growth occurs best in a caring community. Theologian Karl Barth points out that when the New Testament speaks of upbuilding, it "speaks always of the upbuilding of the community. I can identify myself only as I edify the community." And the effective witness and work of Christ in the world comes in the common life of the church.

What gifts of the Spirit exercised in your local community of faith do you most appreciate? How can you encourage those who minister to the body of Christ by the exercise of their gifts?

Question 6. Take care in the consideration and discussion of this question to avoid comments and attitudes that do not contribute to the ultimate upbuilding of the church community. This is not an opportunity to complain or accuse, but to recognize ways the church can be a better Spirit-filled fellowship. For example, a church community that encourages the participation of many gifted people in worship (teaching children, musical skill, drama, dance, intercessory prayer) will honor these gifts given by the Spirit in a way that is not possible in situations where only one or two people are allowed to be involved in the leadership of corporate worship. How does your church encourage people to be involved in the worship service?

Study Four. Bearing Witness. 1 Peter 2:4-12.

Purpose: To show the church as the community of God's people who are God's agents to proclaim salvation and judgment to the world.

Question 4. Biblical evangelism must be church-based evangelism. That is, evangelism should spark church growth, and the life and witness of the church produce evangelism. In this sense the church is both the *agent* and the *goal* of evangelism.

Question 5. The good news which the church proclaims is that in Jesus Christ we are chosen by God and special. This is the answer to the climate of personal worthlessness that marks our culture. By becoming part of God's people, our isolation and loneliness are ended. We are brought into the light which ends our confusion and lack of direction. By God's mercy we experience the forgiveness which sets us free from our shame and guilt.

Question 6. The fallenness of people is made evident by their rejection of God's "chosen and precious" cornerstone, Jesus Christ. They are destined to live outside the mercy and goodness of God. They give in to sinful desires which war against their souls and threaten to destroy them. Finally, the day of God's visitation will come, when God's mercy will no longer be available to them.

Question 7. The New Testament evangelists were faithful verbal witnesses largely because the Christian community was a faithful witness through its common life and its actions in the world. Witness and community go together.

Study Five. Growing the Church. Matthew 13:24-33.

Purpose: To show that the church's numerical growth will be visible, but that spiritual growth is essential to genuine church growth.

Question 2. Until the heads began to form on the wheat, the weeds and the wheat appeared the same. In the early stages of growth the two could not be distinguished from one another.

Question 5. There is something spontaneous about genuine church growth. Normal growth does not depend on successful techniques or programs, although planning has its place. Rather, growth is the normal consequence of spiritual life. What is alive, grows.

Question 6. Church growth is not a matter of bringing to the church that which is necessary for growth. If Christ is there, the seeds of growth are already present. Rather, church growth is a matter of removing the hindrance to growth. The church will naturally grow if it is not limited by unbiblical barriers.

Question 7. The yeast which Jesus refers to was a bit of dough saved from a prior baking and allowed to ferment. It was mixed with the fresh batch of dough, and the yeast permeated the new batch. The dough grew in size, not from any external action, but from the invisible action of the yeast. The church grows in the same way. It is neither programs nor strategy which accounts for genuine church growth. Rather, it is the action of the Spirit permeating the church which accounts for the growth of the kingdom.

Study Six. Organizing the Church. Acts 2:42-47.

Purpose: To understand the role of structure in order for the church to be effective in its life and work.

Question 5. Structure is not the church, just as the wineskin is not the wine. But the structure is necessary in order for the church to live and serve in space and time. Every Christian fellowship must have a culturally appropriate way of doing things at certain times and in certain places.

Question 6. Structuring the church on the basis of discerned tasks and discovered spiritual gifts is one way to a more charismatic/organic church structure which is both more true to the New Testament picture of the church and more functional in a technological society. Properly conceived and followed through, it is a way to circumvent institutionalism and avoid the deadening effects of impersonal programs and promotions.

Commit. Some people are more naturally spontaneous. Others want more planning and organization. In the community of the King, all can benefit from the contributions of different personalities. Organized people learn to be more flexible, possibly more prayerful and dependent on the Lord, and humble. Spontaneous people learn to be more thoughtful, considerate and careful in communication.

Christian Basics Bible Studies from InterVarsity Press

Christian Basics are the keys to becoming a mature disciple. The studies in these guides, based on material from some well-loved books (which can be read along with the studies), will take you through key Scripture passages and help you to apply biblical truths to your life. Each guide has six studies for individuals or groups.

Certainty: Know Why You Believe by Paul Little with Scott Hotaling. Faith means facing hard questions. Is Jesus the only way to God? Why does God allow suffering and evil? These questions need solid answers. These studies will guide you to Scripture to find a reasonable response to the toughest challenges you face.

Character: Who You Are When No One's Looking by Bill Hybels with Dale and Sandy Larsen. Courage. Discipline. Vision. Endurance. Compassion. Self-sacrifice. The qualities covered in this Bible study guide provide a foundation for character. With this foundation and God's guidance, we can maintain character even when we face temptations and troubles.

Christ: Basic Christianity by John Stott with Scott Hotaling. God himself is seeking us through his Son, Jesus Christ. But who is this Jesus? These studies explore the person and character of the man who has altered the face of history. Discover him for the first time or in a new and deeper way.

Christ's Body: The Community of the King by Howard Snyder with Robbie and Breck Castleman. What is God's vision for the church? What is my role? What are my spiritual gifts? This guide helps illumine God's plan for the church and for each of us as a part of it.

Commitment: My Heart—Christ's Home by Robert Boyd Munger with Dale and Sandy Larsen. What would it be like to have Christ come into the home of our hearts? Moving from the living room to the study to the recreation room with him, we discover what he desires for us. These studies will take you through six rooms of your heart. You will be stretched and enriched by your personal meetings with Christ in each study.

Decisions: Finding God's Will by J. I. Packer with Dale and Sandy Larsen. Facing a big decision? From job changes to marriage to buying a house, this guide will give you the biblical grounding you need to discover what God has in store for you.

Excellence: Run with the Horses by Eugene Peterson with Scott Hotaling. Life is difficult. Daily we must choose whether to live cautiously or courageously. God calls us to live at our best, to pursue righteousness, to sustain a drive toward excellence. These studies on Jeremiah's pursuit of excellence with God's help will motivate and inspire you.

Lordship: Basic Discipleship by Floyd McClung with Dale and Sandy Larsen. Have you ever felt like a spiritual failure? Does the Christian life seem like a set of rules that are impossible to follow? This guide contains the biblical keys to true discipleship. By following them you'll be liberated to serve God in every aspect of your life.

Perseverance: A Long Obedience in the Same Direction by Eugene Peterson with Dale and Sandy Larsen. When the going gets tough, what does a Christian do? This world is no friend to grace. God has given us some resources, however. As we grow in character qualities like hope, patience, repentance and joy, we will grow in our ability to persevere. The biblical passages in these studies offer encouragement to continue in the path Christ has set forth for us.

Prayer: Too Busy Not to Pray by Bill Hybels with Dale and Sandy Larsen. There's so much going on—work, church, school, family, relationships: the list is never-ending. Someone always seems to need something from us. But time for God, time to pray, seems impossible to find. These studies are designed to help you slow down and listen to God so that you can respond to him.

Priorities: Tyranny of the Urgent by Charles Hummel. Have you ever wished for a thirty-hour day? Every week we leave a trail of unfinished tasks. Unanswered letters, unvisited friends and unread books haunt our waking moments. We desperately need relief. This guide is designed to help you put your life back in order by discovering what is *really* important. Find out what God's priorities are for you.

Scripture: God's Word for Contemporary Christians by John Stott with Scott Hotaling. What is the place of Scripture in our lives? We know it is important—God's Word to us—but how can it make a difference to us each day? In this guide John Stott will show you the power Scripture can have in your life. These studies will help you make the Bible your anchor to God in the face of the temptation and corruption that are all around.

Spiritual Warfare: The Fight by John White with Dale and Sandy Larsen. As a Christian, you are a sworn foe of the legions of hell. They will oppose you as you obey Christ. Life with Jesus can be an exhilarating and reassuring experience of triumph over evil forces. But the battle never ends. This guide will help you prepare for war.

Witnessing: How to Give Away Your Faith by Paul Little with Dale and Sandy Larsen. If you want to talk about Jesus, but you're not sure what to say—or how to say it—this Bible study guide is for you. It will deepen your understanding of the essentials of faith and strengthen your confidence as you talk with others.

Work: Serving God by What We Do by Ben Patterson with Dietrich Gruen. "I can serve God in church, but can I serve him on the job?" In the factory, in the office, in the home, on the road, on the farm—Ben Patterson says we can give glory to God wherever he calls us. Work, even what seems to us the most mundane, is what God created us for. He is our employer. These studies will show you how your work can become meaningful and satisfying.

Worship: Serving God with Our Praise by Ben Patterson with Dietrich Gruen. Our deepest need can be filled only as we come to our Creator in worship. This is the divine drama in which we are all invited to participate, not as observers but as performers. True worship will transform every part of our lives, and these studies will help you to understand and experience the glory of praising God.